Living in
Roman Times

By Althea
illustrated by Chris and Hilary Evans

Published by Dinosaur Publications

There had been trade between Rome and Britain
for many years before the powerful Romans
decided to add Britain to their Empire.
The Roman army successfully invaded Britain
about forty-three years after the birth of Christ.

Britain remained part of the Roman Empire for nearly four hundred years.

Soldiers from many countries in Europe joined the Roman army. With all the interest in Britain, sailors, merchants and travellers followed the army to Britain in their search for trade. Many of them settled here for good.

We can learn what life was like in Roman Britain by looking at carvings on walls and tombstones.

This tombstone in Chester shows that some people ate sitting on couches with their feet up.
We can see what clothes they wore and what furniture they used.

We know how the Romans cooked by looking at the cooking pots and other kitchen items that have been found. People cooked in pots over a charcoal fire.
Charcoal or wood fires heated their ovens, then the ashes were raked out and the meat or bread was put in to cook.

The Romans were very fond of food, and at that time a man called Apicius wrote two very popular cookery books. From these we can read that they ate many of the things we eat today. But one special recipe was dormice stuffed with minced pork!

Wine and oil were shipped to Britain from France and Italy in pottery bottles called amphorae.

This cooking pot would not have been spoilt by smoke as it was already black.

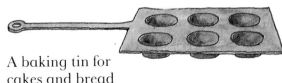

A baking tin for cakes and bread

The Romans were very clean and wanted to
make sure everyone else was as well.
They built public bath houses in every town.
Rich people built their own private bath houses.

The baths, with their hot and cold rooms,
were always a favourite meeting place in the town.
Friends could meet for a chat or exercise and
wrestle in the cold rooms to warm themselves up.
Later, they would sit in the hot rooms and
play board games or gamble with dice.
People living nearby often complained
about the noise coming from the public baths.

After sweating in the hot room, they used this iron 'strigil' to scrape off the dirt. Then they threw cold water over themselves or plunged into a cold bath.

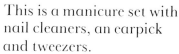

A board game played with counters and dice. We don't know the rules of this game.

Marbles

This is a manicure set with nail cleaners, an earpick and tweezers.
At times, it was fashionable not to have any hair on your face, so people used tweezers to pluck hair from their noses and eyebrows.

This dice was weighted so that it always landed on the same side.

When the invading Romans travelled across
the south of Britain, they were excited
to find a spring of hot water bubbling from
the ground. They built baths over the spring.
The town we now call Bath was built around
the baths. Many visitors came hoping to be cured
of sickness by the water, and to enjoy a holiday.
Greek doctors, dentists and occulists set
up business in Bath and other spa towns
to treat visitors.

The Romans also built a large temple to
Sulis-Minerva. Minerva was the Roman goddess
of healing, and Sul was worshipped by the Celts
as the god of hot springs. Many pilgrims came
to worship at the temple.

You can still visit the Great Bath
though you will not be able to swim in it.
It is lined with huge sheets
made from lead mined in
the Mendip hills.

The Romans built towns all over Britain
with shops and markets very like the
ones we have today.

The farmers in the surrounding countryside
bred animals and grew vegetables, which
they took by donkey or horse and cart
to sell in the local market town.
The richer farmers built large villas.

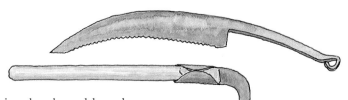

Pruning hook and hand saw
for trimming fruit trees

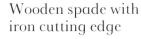

Wooden spade with
iron cutting edge

Iron shears for clipping
wool from sheep. The wool
was later spun and woven
into cloth.

The Roman villa at Chedworth
probably looked like this.
It is open to visitors during
the summer months.
It has two bath houses.

Glass flagon

A strainer made of clay

The potter stamped his own mark on the pot.

The Romans learnt how to blow glass. Some beautiful bottles and pieces of broken glass have been found by people digging for Roman remains. Only the richer Romans had glass windows in their houses. There were glassworks in England but most of the glass was imported from other countries.

There were many potteries in Britain where clay cooking pots and tableware were made. Some pots were made in moulds.

This glass bottle was blown in a square mould. Square bottles did not break so easily when packed together in a crate to bring across the sea.

The potter at work at his wheel.
The kiln was heated by burning charcoal.

17

Rich parents either sent their children
to school or had a tutor to teach them at home.
The books they used were written by hand
on rolls of paper called 'scrolls'.
Paper was expensive to make.
Wooden tablets with writing scratched on
a thin coating of beeswax were used for
everyday messages and for schoolwork.

Stylus for writing
on a tablet

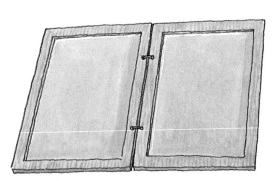

Wooden tablets were tied
together with string to
make a book. The wax
could be heated to melt
the message and the
tablet was used again.

An ink pot and pen for
writing on scrolls

The boy in the picture
is doing his sums
on a tablet.

I II III IV V
VI VII VIII IX X

19

Large town houses and country villas had magnificent mosaic floors. These were made of hundreds of tiny squares of coloured stone, clay or glass, and looked like patterned carpets. In houses with under-floor central heating, the mosaics were nice and warm to walk on in bare feet.

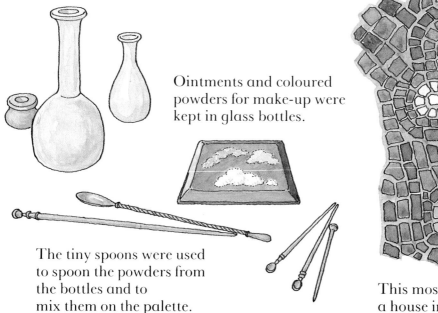

Ointments and coloured powders for make-up were kept in glass bottles.

The tiny spoons were used to spoon the powders from the bottles and to mix them on the palette.

This mosaic was found in a house in Cirencester.

For entertainment, the Romans built large theatres, usually near the edge of town. Touring companies of actors put on pantomimes with a mixture of music and dancing. The players sometimes wore masks like this one as they acted out stories about gods and heroes.

Large crowds came to the theatre to watch wrestling or boxing matches, and cockfighting.

Some towns had huge amphitheatres that were even larger, like a football stadium. Here they held public meetings and army parades.

The theatre at St Albans probably looked like this during a pantomime.

We still have a lot to learn about
what life was like after the Roman army
left Britain, and it was no longer part
of the Roman Empire. Archaeologists are
digging up new clues all the time.

In parts of Britain barbarian armies attacked
and destroyed Roman towns. In other places,
Saxons and the remaining Romans lived
peacefully together. You can visit some
of these places to find out more about
the Romans in Britain.

Text copyright © Althea Braithwaite 1986
Illustrations copyright © Chris and Hilary Evans 1986

Published by Dinosaur Publications,
8 Grafton Street, London W1X 3LA

Dinosaur Publications is an imprint
of Fontana Paperbacks, a division
of the Collins Publishing Group
Printed by Warners of Bourne and London